THE HURT THAT HELPED

ATAVIA BARNES

Self-Published by ASB Consulting Firm | ©COPYRIGHT 2024

Table of Contents

Acknowledgements 5

Dedications 6

What is Hurt? 7

Direct Hurt 12

Components Related to Hurt 14

    Rejection 15

    Abandonment 16

The Five Dimensions of Hurt 17

    Who 18

    What 20

    When 22

    Why 23

    Where 24

Channels Hurt Uses 25

    Word Hurt 26

    Relationship Hurt 29

    Emotional Hurt 30

This is a good place to pray! 34

    Addiction Hurt 37

How does Hurt Affect You? 38

- *Avenues of Hurt* 42
  - *Self-Hurt* 43
  - *Circumstance Hurt* 49
  - *Situation Hurt* 52
  - *Relationship Hurt* 55
- *The Five Dimensions of Healing* 57
  - *The Power of Forgiveness* 58
  - *The Power of Release* 64
- *This is a good place to pray!* 67
- *This is a good place to pray!* 70
- *The Power of Emotional Stability* 71
  - *The Eight Ball* 73
  - *Change your Perspective* 74
  - *Stay Grounded* 74
  - *Don't Suppress* 75
  - *Be Positive* 75
  - *Breathe* 76
  - *Take Care of You* 76
  - *Get Back Up* 77
- *The Fruit of Emotional Stability* 78
  - *The Power of Restoration* 82
  - *The Power of Love* 85
- *Memory is an Enemy to Forgiveness* 88

Healed Perspective 92

This is a good place to pray!!! 101

.... 102

About the Author! 102

References 106

Acknowledgements

I would like to take this time out to thank all of you who worked with me on this project. You all have been with me for a long time. To my editing team, thank you so much for always looking out for me and encouraging me. You all rock.

To my son, Vekarious Barnes, my pride and joy. You always ride with me and have my back. I am so grateful God gave you to me. Love you son. Also, to my family and friends thank you for your love, support, and prayers.

Dedications

This book is dedicated to all of you who have experienced hurt, took it, learned from it, and made it work in your favor.

You Rock!!!

To all my family and friends that walked this journey with me, you were very instrumental in the healing process. Thank you! I know dealing with me was not easy. The assignment was great and you all walked it out with me.

Even when I didn't want to be healed, I wanted to justify the hurt, you stayed, and prayed me through. You know who you are. Thank you for being in my life. I need all of you because you all keep me grounded. I love each one of you to life. Listen, we went from being the victim, and the villain to the Victor!

We Rock!!!

What is Hurt?

Exactly what does it mean to hurt? Hurt has several definitions, and most of them apply to us in some shape, form, or fashion. When dealing with what hurt means, you must also deal with pain.

Hurt means to be detrimental to, distressed, or damaged. Let's also look at other terminology of the meaning of hurt: like wounds, and bleeding (not naturally), but emotionally and spiritually.

Through this journey called life, we will experience some type of hurt; whether it's emotionally, physically, mentally, or financially. Hurt and pain are twins; they work together.

Let's look at pain. Pain has a negative stigma attached to it, but not all results from pain are negative. Pain always look and feel bad, but some pain produces good. If good comes from it, then it was worth the pain.

It's the Hurt that Helped. I once heard someone say, "No pain, no gain." There is some truth to this statement.

Let me give you an example of pain that works for the good.

A woman suffers pain while in labor, but once she pushes through the pain, the result is the gift of life.

It Hurt, but it Produced!!!

Most women don't remember the pain, because the gift of life brings so much joy.

Let's look at some of the definitions for pain: ⁽¹⁾Physical pain – injury to; to inflict, to get hurt, or be hurt ⁽²⁾Suffer pain – of a part of the body; illnesses, dealing with infirmity ⁽³⁾ Emotional anguish – a person's feelings ⁽⁴⁾Character hurt – to be detrimental to; hurt chances of becoming or to hurt chances of promotion or elevation ⁽⁵⁾Financial hurt – lack of money or finances.

All hurt will have some type of effect on you. The depth of the hurt is determined by the five dimensions of hurt, as well as your perspective of the situation that caused the hurt.

Your thoughts of the situation can aggravate your emotions. A willingness to get healed, will cause you to have an open mind to analyze the situation, and look at it from a distinct perspective.

When dealing with hurt, you must have a solid foundation to stand on, to help you maneuver through the process of the hurt. The foundation is the Word of God. Always keep a scripture in your spirit, remember hurt can be tormenting. It can cause you to be oppressed, and depressed.

When dealing with hurt, keep your spirit locked, and loaded with the word of God.

Just in case you are reading this book, and maybe you are experiencing some level of hurt, let me insert some comfort scriptures right here. Just to remind you that the word has whatever it is that you need in the place where you are right now.

"He heals the broken in heart and binds up their wounds." Psalm 147:3. "Many are the afflictions of the righteous: but the LORD delivers him out of them all." Psalm 34:19. "And we know that all things work together for good to them that love God, to them who are the called according to his purpose." Romans 8:28.

These are just a few scriptures to build your faith, just enough for you to see that there is a light at the end of the tunnel. You are not in this alone. It won't be this way always. Hold on, change is coming.

You are going to get through this. What's coming is better than what's been. If you have something to lean on or look forward to, it will help you during the hurt.

If no one else understands you or know what you are going through, God does, and He cares. Often, we look to family and friends for comfort and find none. But, if you look to God, not only will you find comfort, but you will also find peace that surpasses all understanding.

It will overtake you and leave those same people you went to for comfort confused. Why? Because they knew your situation but couldn't comprehend your response.

Remember we must deal with hurt spiritually, emotionally, and naturally to experience complete healing.

Direct Hurt

When dealing with hurt, you must be careful as to where you direct the hurt. Meaning, how you process the hurt or how you channel it. Hurt can affect you psychologically; especially when you don't have an emotional outlet. Emotional outlets are very important when it comes to emotional stability.

What is an emotional outlet? An emotional outlet is a safe place to be able to express your emotions. There are a few ways that you can destress.

Sometimes, it only takes a conversation with someone from your support team, who can walk you through the process of the hurt. Then there are sometimes you can simply do something you like; a hobby or something. When you choose to do something you like, you are distracting yourself from all those negative thoughts that causes the pain.

Learning to channel your emotions in a positive, and constructive way can save you from a lot of emotional damage and wasted time. What do I mean by wasted time? Well, the time you used dwelling on what happened, you could have spent that time writing what happened down in a journal. Tracking your feelings, thoughts, and experiences is a great thing. It's a part of the healing process.

You are channeling all your emotions to paper; the good, the bad, and the ugly. This method allows you to be truthful in expressing your true feelings about the situation or circumstance. It allows you to write in detail the entire story from your lens. In doing this, if you pay attention, you learn a lot about yourself; how you act and react.

Components Related to Hurt

There are two components that contribute to hurt: <u>rejection</u>, and <u>abandonment</u>. Both causes trauma. Let's look more into these components. But first, what is trauma?

Trauma is a psychological, emotional, or physical response to a deeply distressing or disturbing event or series of events that overwhelms an individual's ability to cope. It can have lasting effects on a person's mental, emotional, and physical well-being.

Rejection

What is rejection? Rejection is to refuse to accept, use, or believe in something or someone. It also means not giving someone the love, and attention they want, and are expecting from you. When dealing with rejection, you come to realize that it is the most common emotional wound that we deal with in life.

If we are not careful and aware of our emotions and actions, we self-inflict rejection.

Rejection doesn't operate by itself; the spirit of rejection has two attachments: abandonment and fear.

Abandonment

What is abandonment as it relates to your emotions? Emotional abandonment is a subjective emotional state in which people feel undesired, left behind, insecure, or discarded. It impacts your relationships, your self-esteem, and your sense of security.

Sometimes it manifests itself as issues within relationships, or unhealthy attachments. Also, it can manifest in the form of self-doubt, and delayed dreams because of fear. It can come in the form of toxic connections, self-sabotage, and addictions. Dealing with all the above will cause you to <u>delay</u>, <u>deny</u>, and <u>distract</u>.

In order to deal with emotional abandonment, you must first admit that you have an open wound. I believe in healing spiritually, but I also believe in healing through the means of a psychologist.

The Five Dimensions of Hurt

There are five dimensions of hurt: Who, What, When, Why, and Where. Each dimension has layers.

Just like the five dimensions of hurt, the layers are determined by <u>who</u>, <u>what</u>, <u>when</u>, <u>why</u>, and <u>where</u>. Let's dig into the dimensions and layers.

You will find that coming into the knowledge of what the dimensions and layers consist of, will better help you understand the capacity of the emotional part of you. It will expose the way your heart and your mind process hurt.

This will help you deal with the hurt quicker and more effectively. <u>The layers will reveal how much work is needed to process the hurt.</u>

<u>We will also tap into the channels of hurt. This is the HOW</u> component.

Who

Who hurt you? Was it family, friends, spouse, boyfriend, girlfriend, or co-worker? Was it immediate family, church member, or leadership in church? How close was the family member to you? Was it mom, dad, sister, brother, uncle, auntie, or cousin? Was it by marriage or on one of your parent's side? Was it your best friend or an associate developing into a friend? Was it the co-worker who you confide in? Who was involved in the hurt? Was it directly or indirectly inflicted?

Who, plays a vital part in the level and depth of the hurt you experience. The closer the person is to your heart; the more painful the hurt is.

Who, extends the thickness to the layer. Is it the reason you can't or won't forgive because of who it was? Was it who, that caused you to isolate yourself or put a wall of protection up?

Who, identifies the layer in which the hurt is rooted? The number of who's involved is also a factor.

What I mean is how many were involved in the hurt from the beginning to the end.

Who hurt you, who did you revealed it to? (how did they respond? Did they believe you? Did they defend the villain? What did they do with the information? Did they transition into protection mode? Did they go into warfare? or did they bring other people into the situation)?

Who, is the first dimension of hurt, and it is a very important piece of the puzzle; it determines the layer of the hurt.

David stated in the book of Psalms, "For it was not an enemy that reproached me; then I could have borne it: neither was it he that hated me that did magnify himself against me; then I would have hid myself from him: But it was thou, a man mine equal, my guide, and mine acquaintance." Psalm 55:12 – 13.

What

What, is the second dimension of hurt. What did they do? What did they say? What was involved? What happened? What was the root cause of the hurt? What were you doing when it happened? What was your initial reaction? What was the purpose of this hurt?

You can't ask what without expressing how. How did they do it? How did it come about? How did you respond? How did you handle it? or how are you handling it? What stage of the process are you in now? The second layer consists of situations and circumstances.

You can't forgive someone unless you have a what, which is the explanation of the situation. What explains why you are forgiving that person or you are forgiving the situation. What also helps explain the depth of the situation. What is the subject matter, and the story is the supporting information for the subject.

When telling a story about a situation, you will always get the questions of what happened? When did it happen? Who else was involved or who else was there? How did this happen? Why did this happen? Situations will always have these questions.

When

When, is the third dimension of hurt. When did it happen? What age were you when this happened? What season of your life were you in when it happened? Where was your mindset when it happened? This dimension carries layers of the hurt.

When, determines how the situation is handled. Also, when can determine the depth of the hurt. Is this a child-hood hurt you're dealing with? What era of child-hood were you in? Were you a toddler, preschooler, teenager, young adult or were you fully grown when this occurred?

This dimension is important because it determines how you process the hurt. Children process hurt differently than adults. Children deal with inner conflict; they don't understand how to properly place their emotions. Adults that choose not to deal with the hurt, play the blame game. Everyone who they let in, they try to make them pay for what happened to them, which is a temporary fix, but not healing.

Why

Why, is the fourth dimension of hurt. Why did this happen? Why did this happen to me? Why did it happen like that? Why, can go on forever, and after every situation there are questions. The questions often seek responsibility. You are trying to seek answers to see where you fit in this situation.

You try to analyze your part in it, whether you were right or wrong. Were you responsible for their actions? Are you innocent or guilty? Why! will mess with your self-esteem.

Asking why eliminates confusion and positions you for the healing process.

Where

Where is the fifth dimension of hurt. Where did it happen? Were you at home, at grandma's house, or were you at a friend's house? Were you at school? Were you at church? At Work? Were you at a ball game? Where was your physical location? Where was the location of your heart? Your mind? Where were you when you experienced the hurt?

These five dimensions are key in your hurt because they create what we call memory. Location is also very important because it reveals the sting of the situation.

Learning the five dimensions exposes exactly what level of hurt you are dealing with, and why you are dealing with it. They help you put the hurt in perspective.

Channels Hurt Uses

The channels that hurt uses can cause us to react negatively. We put up a wall of defense and won't allow anyone in or out. Believe it or not, these channels are everyday common outlets.

Some of the most used channels are: words, relationships, emotional, physical and addictions. They can implement rejection, isolation, hatred, and bitterness if not dealt with properly.

Word Hurt

What exactly is word hurt? It is the meaning of a word or expression; the way in which a word or expression can be interpreted. Word hurt can be inflicted directly and indirectly. Directly, when you address the person. Indirectly, when the person is addressed through third party (other people's conversation), which is gossip.

Words carry weight and hold power. Words can be both positive and negative. They can uplift or tear down, encourage or bash.

Word hurt consists of words that <u>discount</u>, <u>demean</u>, and <u>devalue</u> words and statements. Words that discount are invalidations, and challenges, that reduce the value to your intellect or thoughts.

Words that demean are character assassinations that are designed to induce shame, embarrassment, or guilt. This hurt states or implies that you are somewhat a failure. Also, it relies on forced self-reflection that will cause you to self-sabotage.

Words that devalue are threats of abandonment and exile which include phrases that indicate the cutting of ties.

Words are powerful and carry influence. Therefore, we must be careful with our words. Words can hurt or heal, destroy, or create. Words are powerful, but also important and necessary. They are so powerful that when we speak the earth must yield to our words.

Some people call it the law of attraction. I call it walking in the power and authority that God has given to us as His children.

> *Genesis 1:26 says: "And God said, let us make man in our image, after our likeness: and let them have dominion over the fish of the sea, and over the fowl of the air and over the cattle and over all the earth, and over every creeping thing that creeps upon the earth.*
>
> *"Then God went on to say in Romans 4:17 "As it is written, I have made thee a father of many nations, (here, he was talking to Abraham), before him whom he believed, even God, who quickens the dead, and call those things which be not as though they were."*

You can frame your future by the words you speak. By words, God created the heaven and the earth. He simply spoke let there be, and there was.

Words can be bitter or sweet, they can be used as a <u>weapon</u> or <u>medicine</u>. As a weapon, words can be both negative and positive: negatively when we use our words to gossip, lie, kill the character of others, sabotage or to gain popularity. Positive when we are in warfare or intercession.

Words in the form of medicine is when we use our words to bring healing.

Words have the power to encourage, bring a calm to the storm, and words of faith will silence the enemy. Words carry influence, they can persuade you towards evil or good.

We must deal with all channels of hurt. If we continue to let hurt be the driving force in our lives, we will continue the cycle of hurt people hurting people.

Relationship Hurt

Relationship hurt deals with heart matters. It's when you experience heart hurt by way of relationship, whether it is family, friends, co-workers at the workplace, or romance.

It doesn't matter how you look at it, hurt is a part of the ship. Relationship hurt is one of the most common, and popular hurts. This hurt involves people and is involved in all the other hurts. This hurt can also be the most dangerous hurt because hurt people hurt other people.

Also, like word hurt, this hurt is one of the causes of isolation, rejection, and bitterness. It produces trust issues. Relationship hurt cuts deep and wide.

This hurt causes new relationships to be charged with past due debts from old relationships. This hurt will cause you not to trust anyone, therefore there is a great possibility that you can miss out on great relationships that God is trying to give you as a gift.

Emotional Hurt

Emotional hurt is suffering psychologically. There are different components of emotional hurt: rejection, rumination, loneliness, distress, self-guilt, failure, and low self-esteem.

Rejection is the denial of acceptance, exclusion from, whether from a group, an interaction, information, communication, or emotional intimacy. It is probably the most painful, and the most neglected, yet one of the most common emotional wounds from which we suffer.

Rejection victimizes its prey by causing them to feel worthless and unwanted. It causes you to question your self-worth, have self-pity, and cause self-inflictions.

Rejection taunts you with what feels like one failure after another, to provoke you to give up.

Also, rejection, and the fear of rejection play a major part in the development of our character.

> *A broken spirit is a major component for rejection.*
>
> *Proverbs 15:13 says: "A joyful heart makes a cheerful face, but when the heart is sad, the spirit is broken. One of the characteristics of rejection is a broken spirit.*
>
> *Proverbs 17:22 says: "A joyful heart is good medicine, but a broken spirit dries up the bones." A broken spirit brought about by rejection can dry up or wax cold.*
>
> *In Proverbs 18:14: The spirit of a man can endures his sickness, but a broken spirit who can bear? If you don't deal with rejection, there is no chance for healing to take place.*

Some of the characteristics of rejection working in your life is that you compare your circumstances or situations with others. You feel like you never seem to measure up. You feel alone, no one understands you or what you are experiencing.

Sometimes, you feel like you have missed out on some of life's opportunities. It's hard to convince you of your worth. Acknowledgement is very important to you. You consistently seek approval or affirmation.

You're easily offended and always trying to prove yourself.

> *Rumination is repetitively going over a thought or a problem without completion. This focuses attention on the symptoms of one's distress, and on its probable causes and consequences, but never explore the options of solution(s).*

It fosters negative thinking and will trap you in a cycle if you are not careful. Also, it causes your ability to problem solve or forgive to be impaired. This can be dangerous as it is a replay of the situation or circumstance, but never allows you to go past that memory. Rumination can stop or delay the potential for healing.

Loneliness is a complex and usually unpleasant emotional response to isolation. It typically includes anxious feelings. It can be felt even when surrounded by other people.

If you are not careful, loneliness will cause you to lower your standards and accept anything.

You become vulnerable which causes you to become a target. Even in accepting anything, the loneliness does not go away, it's just suppressed temporarily.

This emotion is most experienced when you are in the waiting season. You've sought the Lord about something and the answer has not manifested yet, so you become anxious and your patience runs out. It feels like confirmation from the Lord becomes weak and most people don't understand your struggle.

Defeat loneliness with not just the word of God or prayer; but put action in place by obtaining a hobby or get out of the house. Go hang out with friends to shift your mind set. Give God something to work with. Be careful with loneliness because the spirit of depression is attached to it.

> ## *This is a good place to pray!*

Lord, I come to your throne of grace, casting all my anxiety on You because You care for me. Lord, I come confessing that I deal with the spirit of loneliness.

Lord, I cry out to You today to send strong deliverance. In my defense, Lord I ask that You give me a strategy to not only deal with this spirit, but to destroy it, and cast this spirit out of my life.

Teach me how to identify this spirit and I will use that knowledge to defeat it. Help me O God to shift my mind set regarding the situation or circumstance that triggered this spirit.

Lord grant me power to destroy the attack of the enemy, for You said in your word that you would teach my hands to war and my fingers to battle. I desire to be delivered from loneliness. I know You are with me and for me.

I will decree and declare the word of the Lord over my life every time I feel this spirit trying to come over me. Lord, I thank You and praise You in your son Jesus name I pray, Amen!

Distress is dealing with anxiety, and it will cause you to isolate yourself. If you are not careful when you are emotionally distressed, you will create a fantasy world to escape reality. Dealing with distress will cause you to be easily stressed, and your patience wears very thin. Every little thing will get on your nerves.

Also, when dealing with being distressed, you feel drained all the time. It's like you've been in a fight and you've lost. Whenever you feel distress, take a step back and gather yourself, so you can think clearly. Whatever you do, don't make the next move without the counsel of God's wisdom.

Failure is the <u>appearance</u> of the lack of success. If you experience failure once, it makes that in which you failed and all future goals seem unattainable. It distorts your perception of your own abilities. It will lead you to unconscious self-sabotage.

Failure is where knowledge is built. The experience of the last failure develops the understanding of the *failure which produces wisdom. Believe it or not, failure is a part of success.*

This is the perfect time to go back and get that dream, write the vision, and remember what the failure was, and build from there. This time you know what not to do and what to do.

Low self-esteem is your thought process of yourself. Most people who deal with low self-esteem have either experienced trauma, been rejected, abandoned, there was no affirmation during the development years, or they experienced failure.

What happened to you or what you went through does not determine your value. Those were experiences to build you for greatness.

You have to be willing to allow God into that place to heal and move you forward.

Addiction Hurt

Addiction hurt is the hurt that affects the entire world of the person with the addiction. Those who are connected to this person also feel the effects of the addiction. Addictions are not just substance abuse; it can be alcohol, food, shopping, sexual, stealing, etc.

This hurt affects finances, causes isolation, secrecy, lies, and enabling through hope (meaning because you have faith for this person or you have hope of deliverance, you enable them in their struggle). This is a stronghold that must be dealt with as a family.

Remember love cannot cure this illness, it's a part of the cure, but not the cure. If you are not careful, love will cause you to become the enabler.

I know some people who prayed, asked God to take the taste and habit from them, and it happened instantly. Then, there are some people who had to go through a process to get delivered.

How does Hurt Affect You?

Let's talk about some characteristics of hurt. Again, hurt people hurt other people. They transfer their inner anger onto other people. I call this the <u>victim</u> and the <u>villain</u>.

Hurt people interpret every word spoken to them through their hurt. Therefore, what we consider an ordinary word is often misinterpreted to mean something negative. Hurt people interpret every action through their hurt. Their emotional hurt causes them to suspect wrong motive, and intent behind other people's actions towards them. Hurt people often carry around a suspicious spirit, and they have a tough time entering a trusting relationship.

Hurt people have the emotional maturity of the age of when they received their (un-dealt with) hurt.

Hurt people are often frustrated and depressed. They can't seem to get past their irritation or the pressure of the emotions.

Hurt people often attempt to medicate themselves with excessive entertainment, drugs, alcohol, pornography, sexual relationships, or hobbies to forget the hurt, not knowing this only suppresses it.

The hurt will remain and come up again. You must repeat what you did to suppress it in the first place, which causes your reactions to the hurt to become habitual.

Now, you have started adding layers to the hurt already present. Hurt people are often self-absorbed with their own hurt; they are unaware that they are hurting other people.

Hurt affects you in many ways. If you are not careful, it can, and if not dealt with will change you. Hurt isolates you, controls your reactions, installs a firewall (you won't allow anyone in or out, and you get irritated, frustrated, and mad when you are not in control.) You call it a security system, but really, it's your hurt guard.

Hurt traps your thoughts; it puts a demand on your attitude, and it ultimately changes who you are. Hurt not only affects you, but it affects those around you, your surroundings, and even affects relationships.

Hurt will drive people away from you, and will cause people to only tolerate you. Hurt is so aggressive that if you don't deal with the hurt in a timely fashion, it will start to affect not only your emotions, but your mental state, and your all-around health.

Hurt is a monster that is more dangerous than it appears. Hurt will try to hide behind what we call a mask.

> *Hurt will use a smile, religion, careers or whatever it can use to keep you in captivity.*

When you look at yourself, you see the mask you have put on, and now you have worn it so long, that to you, the mask looks like you. Hurt has changed the way you see yourself, and to you, you are alright because the mask looks and feels like you, but guess what? That's not you.

The deception is that the hurt has convinced you that you're okay, however, those who are in your space can see the mask.

But watch this, those that see the mask remind you that it is a mask and offer help to remove it.

They are also the same ones who experience the venom of the hurt.

Avenues of Hurt

There are four avenues of hurt that will give us a synopsis of what causes us to play into the role of being a victim, and villain.

- **Self-Hurt** *(the law of sowing and reaping).*
- **Circumstance Hurt** *(dreams, visions, and desires).*
- **Situation Hurt** *(something happened)*
- **Relationship Hurt** *(family, friends, spouse, or courtship).*

As you notice relationship hurt is in here twice. It is listed as a channel that hurt uses, and an avenue of hurt. So, hurt really uses relationships. All of the hurts play a part in the emotional component in each one of us. Let's look at each one of them starting with self-hurt.

Self-Hurt

The Victim & The Villain
(Genesis 27 & 29)

A victim is a person who has been hurt or damaged. A victim can also be someone who is deceived or cheated, as by his or her own emotions.

The victim and the villain can also be someone who feels the need to be accountable for the mistakes of others, or who is turned into the victim by someone else.

A villain is a hurt person hurting other people, transferring their inner hurt onto other people, while continuing to play the victim.

They use their hurt to justify their actions and reactions.

Let's look at a story in the bible that displays the Victim and the Villain. Genesis 29:25 says: And it came to pass, that in the morning, behold, it was Leah. And he said to Laban, "What is this thou hast done unto me?" did not I serve with thee for Rachel? wherefore then hast thou beguiled me?

Let's go back and build a case!

> *Let's look at Genesis 27:5 – 8. And Rebekah heard when Isaac spoke to Esau his son. And Esau went to the field to hunt for venison, and to bring it. And Rebekah spoke unto Jacob her son, saying, Behold, I heard thy father speak unto Esau thy brother, saying, bring me venison, and make me savory meat, that I may eat, and bless thee before the LORD before my death. Now therefore, my son, obey my voice according to that which I command thee.*

Jacob is a <u>victim by obedience</u>, but at the same time he was a <u>villain by desire</u>.

Jacob had a desire to be blessed by his father, and that led to deception by the instructions of his mother. <u>Desire</u> and <u>deception</u> followed Jacob. He flees to his uncle's house where he will not only reap what he sowed, but he will discover the spirit of his mother's house. He was in a new place dealing with the same spirit.

> *Genesis 29: 11 & 18 says: Jacob met Rachel at the well, kissed her, and lifted his voice, and wept. And Jacob loved Rachel; and said, I will serve thee seven years for Rachel thy younger daughter.*

When you play the game, you must be on guard always, or the game will play you. Remember, Jacob served seven years for Rachel, but there was a problem, not with the service, but with the customs.

In the days of old, it was not customary for the younger daughter to marry before the elder. So, because of customs, Laban gave Jacob, the eldest, Leah instead of Rachel.

Once again, Jacob is the victim, but this time it's because he has just entered a season of reaping what you sow.

On the other hand, Leah enters that same season, but for a different reason. She was not reaping what she sowed, but she is forced into a season called the victim and the villain. Leah was forced to be the victim because of customs.

Some of us are forced to be victims because we won't allow God to touch that place of hurt that we are holding onto. She was glad to be this victim because she had challenges, but she also had the man (just like we are glad to be the victim of our circumstances and call it justification).

The bible says she was tender eyed, meaning she was not pleasant to the eye. Leah became a victim because of what she knew. She knew she was not the chosen one. She knew she was only given to Jacob because of customs.

She knew that Jacob loved Rachel, and that there was no place in his heart for her. Rachel held the capacity of his heart. Leah was married to him seven years, and his heart never changed.

Also, when Leah was the only wife, she was bearing. The bible says the Lord saw that Leah was hated so, that He opened her womb.
In this story, there are three victims, and three villains! Leah, Jacob, and Rachel are victims. Laban, Leah, and Jacob are villains.

Laban was the victim because he knew Leah's situation, and as a father, he decided to help her using the custom. His emotional attachment to his daughter drew out obligation, therefore becoming the villain (he became victim out emotional attachment and villain out of obligation).

You must watch where your loyalty lies, because wrong motives behind loyalty will produce bad decisions that alter your life, and hurt others in the process.

Jacob took something that wasn't his, and in return he was given something he didn't want. He was the villain, and became the victim. He reaped what he'd sown. Leah was a victim by rejection. She had challenges and her challenges caused her to become a villain by desire. She was forced into something. She had to watch what she really wanted and couldn't have. True love from a man who didn't have the capacity to accept what she was trying to give.

In opening Leah's womb, she conceived, and bore a son, and she called his name Reuben: for she said, Surely the LORD hath looked upon my affliction; now, therefore my husband will love me.

And she conceived again, and bare a son; and said, Because the LORD hath heard I was hated, he hath therefore given me this son also: and she called his name Simeon.

And she conceived again, and bare a son; and said, now this time will my husband be joined unto me, because I have born him three sons: therefore, was his name called Levi. And she conceived again, and bare a son: and she said, now will I praise the LORD: therefore, she called his name Judah; and left bearing. She ceased from having babies for a season.

The healing for Leah came when she finally realized, I've been giving emotional power to the wrong person, and the love I have to give should be vertical and then horizonal. She shifted with the last baby. Healing will cause you to shift. She is no longer the victim or the villain, but the victor.

Circumstance Hurt

Desire
(1 Samuel 1)

Elkanah had two wives, Hannah and Peninnah. Peninnah had children, but Hannah had none. Elkanah went up yearly to Shiloh to worship and to sacrifice unto the Lord. When the time came for Elkanah to offer his sacrifice, he gave Peninnah his wife and to all her sons and daughters, portions. But to Hannah, he gave a worthy portion (meaning more than), for he loved Hannah, but the Lord had shut up her womb. And her adversary also provoked her sore, to make her fret because her womb was shut.

Every year when they went to Shiloh, she provoked her, and therefore, Hannah wept and did not eat. Her husband was concerned as to why she was crying and not eating. He stated the fact that he was better to her than ten sons.

Peninnah was a victim and the villain. She was a victim because she knew that Elkanah's love for Hannah was more intense, and there was nothing she could do about it. She was a villain because she knew Hannah's desire and she used her children to vex Hannah.

Hannah was a victim and a villain. She was a victim because of her desire to have a child. This desire was so strong that it started affecting her emotionally. If you study the signs of depression, you will find crying and loss of appetite are two of them among others. It affects your emotions to the point you cry and you don't want to eat.

Also, it affects your sight. Hannah couldn't see what she had because she was looking at what she didn't have. She was a villain because of her desire to have a child.

This desire overrode everything about Hannah, her quality of life was affected. The scripture states that she was in bitterness of soul.

Last, but not least, her emotional state caused concern for her husband, and he was hurt because he didn't know what to do to please Hannah. This made Elkanah a victim to her desire as well.

Elkanah was the victim because he wanted to make his wife happy but didn't know how. He tried with money, gifts, and attention, but that would not satisfy her desire for a child. He was a villain because of how he treated Hannah with all the attention, to the point of provoking Peninnah to be a villain.

Something happened in the course of all the hurt in this family. Hannah's desire caused a shift in her spirit, and this shift is what God was waiting on. Hannah shifted her perspective, rose up, and went to the temple, weeping to the point that Eli, the priest thought she was drunk. She shifted into prayer, made a vow, and God honored her prayer.

Remember, God never produces anything in the earth unless there's a need. God needed a prophet to be born in the earth at the same time Hannah desperation provoked her to make a vow. The vow released the miracle, and in return the miracle fulfilled the need.

Situation Hurt

Something Happened
(Genesis 16)

Abram's wife Sarai was well up in age, and she had no children because she was barren. Sarai offered her handmaid, whose name was Hagar, to her husband, Abram, that she might bare children in her stead. When Sarai told this idea to her husband, he listened to the voice of Sarai. Abram married Hagar and once they were married, she conceived, she looked with contempt on Sarai (regarding her as in significant because of her infertility), she despised her.

And Sarai said to Abram, may the responsibility for the wrong done to me by the arrogant behavior of Hagar be upon you. May the Lord judge between you and me. But Abram said unto Sarai, "Look, your maid is entirely in your hands, and subject to your authority; do as you please with her." Sarai treated her harshly, and humiliated her, and Hagar fled from her.

And the angel of the Lord found her by a fountain of water in the wilderness on the way to Shur. And he said, Hagar, Sarai's maid, where did you come from? and where are you going? She said, I fled from the face of Sarai.

*The angel of the L*ORD *said to her, return to thy mistress, and submit thyself under her hands. And the angel of the L*ORD *said to her, I will multiply thy seed exceedingly, that it shall not be numbered for multitude.*

*And the angel of the L*ORD *said to her, Behold, you are with child, and shall bear a son, and shall call his name Ishmael, because the L*ORD *hath heard thy affliction.*

Sarai became a victim by her desire to give Abram a child, and a villain by dragging everyone else into her foolishness. Abram was a victim when he hearkened unto Sarai's voice, and a villain by trying to accommodate Sarai emotions (Hagar is your handmaid, due what you will).

Forget the fact that Sarai pulled Hagar into this, forget the fact that she is pregnant, forget the fact that she is his wife. Forget all of that because she is just a vessel that you two are using to fulfill a desire). <u>It wasn't the promise, it was the desire.</u>

Hagar became a victim when she was chosen and conceived, but became the villain when she became disrespectful, and arrogant because she was with child. Ishmael became a victim at conception, because of the motive behind the conception as well as his mother disrespect to Sarai.

Relationship Hurt

Because I was Chosen (Genesis 37& 39)

There was a seventeen-year-old by the name of Joseph, he was the youngest of all of Jacob children. Jacob loved Joseph more than all his children, because he was the son of his old age.

Jacob made Joseph a distinctive multicolored coat. His brothers saw that their father loved Joseph more; so, they hated him. Joseph had a dream of rulership, and he told his brothers, and this caused their hate to intensify.

Joseph had another dream of rulership, and again told his brothers, and this time his father, but his father rebuked him, and said to him in disbelief, "What is the meaning of this dream that you have dreamed? Are you saying that we are actually going to bow down to the ground in respect before you?"

Even though his father rebuked him, he kept the words of Joseph in mind wondering about the meaning. Later, Jacob sent Joseph to check on his brothers to make sure everything was okay.

While trying to locate his brothers, they saw him from a distance, and began to plot to kill him.

Joseph was put in the pit, sold to the Midianites for twenty shekels of silver, then sold into slavery to Potiphar, an officer of Pharaoh and the captain of the royal guard.

When Joseph was falsely accused and ends up in prison, he finally reached his destination to the palace. A dream put him in prison, but a dream also got him out. Joseph was a victim because of the love his father had for him.

Also, his dream caused him to be a victim, but because of how he handled the process, another dream caused him to be the victor. You have to be careful with the avenues of hurt, because they will cause you to become the victim and the villain.

Now that we have reviewed the problem(s), let's look at the solution(s).

The Five Dimensions of Healing

There are five dimensions of healing that I want to deal with.

- *The Power of Forgiveness*
- *The Power of Release*
- *The Power of Emotional Stability and being Whole*
- *The Power of Restoration*
- *The Power of Love*

The Power of Forgiveness

What is forgiveness? Forgiveness is the <u>action</u> or <u>process</u> of forgiving or being forgiven. To deal with forgiveness, you must deal with two components: <u>action</u> and <u>process</u>.

Action is the accomplishment of a thing usually over a period of time, or in stages. Process is a series of actions, or operations in execution to bring about or to bring to an end.

Sometimes forgiveness is instant and other times, it's a process. Why? Because when dealing with hurt, most people must have time to process the hurt, and evaluate their emotions. When forgiving, you must make a conscious decision to stop feeling anger towards the person(s) who hurt you.

You must eliminate the blame game. Also, remember forgiveness is not something you do for other people. You do it for you to get well and move forward. Forgiveness is essential for spiritual growth. That's the reason why the enemy tries to entrap you in the hurt.

To truly forgive, one must be willing to give up resentment, or claim to requital which is retaliation. There's a fight that you must fight; because the spirit of justification is strong when it comes to forgiveness.

You must be willing to cease to feel resentment against what you call the enemy; because you are trying to justify your emotions, and you must be willing to grant forgiveness.

Remember, this is your power that you are taking back when you are willing to grant forgiveness; and you are opening opportunities to be forgiven. The power of forgiveness is strategic within itself. The power of it transforms anger, and hurt into healing, and potential: a fresh start, rebuilding possibilities, and restoration.

It also helps you to overcome the feeling of depression, anxiety, and conflict, thus experiencing peace. It empowers you to make a conscious decision not only to forgive, but to also release, and let go. You have now taken full control of your emotions and let go control of the situation.

"I choose to forgive, release, and let go." That statement is so powerful. The true test of forgiveness is when you have to face <u>what was</u>, meaning you may see that person again, or there's an instance where the situation is presented again.

The passing of the test is that you are in a different place with a different mindset, and you are healed, so you respond accordingly.

Some may ask the question; how do I forgive? Is forgiveness even possible? You don't know what I experienced, what I went through, who did this to me, and how deep the hurt is. You really don't know.

My answer is, you really don't know how much God loves, and cares about you. He cares about the hurt and wants to heal you from the hurt.

> *What you must understand is that the actual situation is in the past, the hurt you are dealing with is a memory, and in that memory, you don't see justice, and because your mindset is still that of they should pay for what they did, you store that memory in hopes of payment.*

Remember, the experience of the hurt even though it's painful, and maybe still fresh, is your past. By the time I make this statement, it is no longer now, but was. It's now nothing more than a memory, thought, or feeling that you are carrying and holding onto.

These thoughts of anger, resentment, and hatred will cause you to lose your power, if you allow these thoughts to continue to occupy space in your mind. The more aged these thoughts become, the more of you is affected. I know what you are thinking!!! Forgiveness is easier said than done. To some extent, I do agree, but if you really want to be healed, your efforts are very necessary.

Take your life as a story with chapters. Just because the character started in the first chapter; doesn't mean they will make it to the second chapter. Remember, every chapter of your life has purpose, and believe it or not, hurt was already formulated in the chapters of your life.

In life, you will have heroes and villains. All of them have purpose in helping you reach destiny.

Embrace all of them because they are employees. They work for you.

Some hurt is more aggressive than others. Some hurt you are able to forgive, and move on because we make the decision to forgive, but then there are some hurts that we have to do as the scripture says in Matthew 17:21 "Howbeit this kind goes not out but by prayer and fasting." The word goes means continually because God already knew hurt would come more than once.

One thing I have noticed about hurt, is that the reason you can't get completely healed from hurt, is because before we decided to forgive and release, we allowed hurt to pile on top of hurt.

Now, your emotions are all over the place, and now you are dealing with intent, and motive. This taps into our relationships, because going into a new relationship, we often look for the characteristics of what we experienced, thus putting up a firewall. So, our new relationship(s) start out barren. It can't bear any fruit.

Three important components that are very necessary when walking through the process of forgiveness are:

guard your ear gates, guard the "who" in your space, and time. The sensitivity of the process is very detrimental.

Guard your ear gates. If you have shared your hurt with others, they will feed the hurt by justifying it, and giving bad advice. Not intentionally, but because they love you, and they are experiencing the hurt with you. Which leads to my next point. Watch who you tell about your hurt, because if you forgive the person, sometimes the one(s) you told will have a tough time forgiving them. This is especially important regarding marriage. So, if the person can't help you, then don't tell them because you bind them up with anger, and resentment.

Time is a very important factor regarding forgiveness. The longer you wait to deal with the hurt, the harder it will be to forgive. Quiet time is also necessary. Get in a quiet place so you can deal with your thoughts, and your heart.

The Power of Release

Now that you have completed the process of forgiveness, let's move forward with the releasing process. When you forgive, you must also release.

Exactly what does it mean to release? To release is to relieve from something that confines, burdens, or oppressed. It also means to move from one's normal position to assume another position. You adjusted their space in your life because of the hurt.

You have forgiven them, and now you are releasing them, but with the knowledge of the past, you readjust their position.

Also, release means to discharge from obligation, or responsibility. Forgiveness and release work together. I think an effective way to release someone is to deal with what forgiveness is <u>NOT</u>.

Forgiveness doesn't mean you are excusing the other person's actions. Forgiveness doesn't mean you need to tell the person that he or she is forgiven. Forgiveness doesn't mean you shouldn't have any more feelings about the situation.

Forgiveness doesn't mean there is nothing further to work out in the relationship. Forgiveness doesn't mean you should forget the incident ever happened. Forgiveness doesn't mean you have to continue to include the person in your life. Forgiveness isn't something you do for the other person.

By forgiving, you are accepting the reality of what happened, and finding a way to live in a state of resolution with it. This can be a gradual process, and it doesn't have to include the person(s) you are forgiving.

Forgiveness requires feelings willing to forgive, meaning your emotions have to submit to the decision you made. In the process of releasing, you must deal with you. Now is the time to be open, and honest with self.

Think about the situation, or circumstance that hurt you, and process it through acceptance, and acknowledgment.

- o *Accept that it happened.*
- o *Accept how you felt about it.*
- o *Accept your reactions*
- o *Acknowledge the reality of what occurred, and how you were affected.*

Acknowledge the results of the experience by asking yourself the following questions:

- o *What did you learn about yourself or about your needs and boundaries?*
- o *Now that you survived, did you grow from it?*
- o *Are you a better person because of it?*

Now deal with the other person. All humans are flawed and can operate from limited beliefs which is an emotional impact of an experience, or a frame of reference; a complex lens through which they view a situation.

- o *What do you think they were dealing with at the time of the incident?*
- o *Was the hurt intentional?*
- o *Why do you think the person went about it in such a hurtful way?*

> *This is a good place to pray!*

Lord, I admit I am struggling to forgive (insert name(s) in my own strength.

Please help me to forgive and release them. Lord, I pray that you would take the sting out of the hurt so I can properly heal. Help me to truly forgive and release them.

Heal my mind that the memory of the hurt no longer provokes a reaction out of me. Heal my heart that I may love them again. Help me to forgive them, so I won't develop layers of hurt in my heart that would lead to bitterness. I want to be emotionally stable and I want to be whole.

Lord, forgive me for bringing other people into this hurt place. Forgive me for spewing out venom regarding the person and the situation.

Forgive me for my motives and intent to justify my reactions to the hurt. Forgive me Father for holding on to this hurt for as long as I have held on. I want to be free from this and I want them to be free. Help me God to free both of us.

> *Lord, heal all parties involved. The victim, villain, and the innocent bystander. In the name of Jesus! Amen!*

Forgive and release puts the final seal on the hurt you experienced. You will still have the memory, but not the sting, therefore you will no longer be bound by it.

Working through your feelings and learning what you need to do to strengthen your boundaries is very important, this will help you better deal with what may come later.

There's both a natural and a spiritual component when dealing with forgiveness and release. This is not a one-time process because life happens and it happens repeatedly.

Forgiveness and release is a spiritual exercise. It's impossible to truly forgive without God's help. Here is a couple of tips that could be therapeutic moving forward. Remember even after the process, the enemy will present the past.

Keep a journal around and even though you may have written it down before, show the enemy you have tenacity and write it again.

Let the enemy know I am determined to move forward freely. Write down the name of the person(s) you need to forgive.

Write down the things in which you need forgiveness (how many people have you hurt because of your hurt?).

Surrender time!!! The time has come to let go of the deep, deep desire to get even with them, to expose them, or retaliate against them.

> *This is a good place to pray!*

Lord, I am bringing my will under Your will, and Your power. I give my rights to You to get even with (insert name(s).

I make a commitment that when those thoughts, feelings, and emotions come over me again, I will release them. I will not babysit them. I admit the feelings are real, but I choose not to be controlled by them any longer. Instead, I will dwell on the good things I have learned from this experience.

Lord, help me to kill my past that my future may live. For we put You in remembrance of Your word that states in Romans 8:28. And we know that all things, the good, the bad, and the ugly work together for good to them that love God, to them who are the called according to his purpose.

Lord, we love you, we praise you, and we bless your Holy name. We trust you, and we give your name praise, glory, and honor. In the name of Jesus, I pray! Amen!

The Power of Emotional Stability

Emotional stability is the state or quality of being stable in your emotions. It refers to a person's ability to remain calm when faced with pressure or stress. Emotional stability is very necessary because:

- *Those who live by emotions live without principle.*
- *You cannot be spiritual or walk in the spirit and be led by emotions.*
- *Emotions won't go away, but you can learn to manage them.*
- *You can have emotions, but you can't always rely on them.*
- *Make emotional maturity a primary goal in your life.*

During the healing process, emotional stability has to be developed as you are transitioning.

During this transition, you are fighting with you. (should I, can I, I have a right, they were wrong, I wasn't bothering anyone, why me?).

Emotions, emotions, emotions. You are dealing with your past, present, and future all at once. You are trying to move from your past, walking in healing now, so, you will have a future to look forward too.

You are between the stages of hurt, confusion, confession, forgiveness, and release. WOW!!! That's a lot at once. And all are decisions.

The Eight Ball

The eight-ball practice is to help stabilize your emotions. Controlling your emotions is a skill that takes practice, awareness and a lot of discipline and self-control.

Emotional stability plays a significant role in being whole. The eight ball says let's practice this:

Change your Perspective

- *Perspective is everything. If you view something as an attack, chances are you'll become defensive.*
- *Catch the lesson in every experience. Practice looking at the situation as an observer. Imagine you are the mediator in the confrontation. Look at the situation from the other person's perspective.*

Know you are in Control

- *Become aware of your thought patterns. Doing this will cause you to gain control of your thoughts and intentionally calm them. Become aware, assess the problem, then take the proper action.*

Stay Grounded

- *Find a scripture that is applicable to the situation, and put it in your spirit, so when that memory tries to come around, you can regurgitate the word of God.*

> o *Posture yourself in prayer and get around some positive people. Also, don't allow anybody else's perception to sway you. Stand firm.*

Don't Suppress

> o *Learn to listen to your emotions. Don't ever store or bottle up these strong emotions, or they will more than likely end in an explosive outburst of emotions. This is where we say something we don't mean or do something we often regret.*

Be Positive

> o *Reflect on what you're grateful for, and why. Choose two to three affirmations that represent your values, and goals.*
>
> o *The repetition will influence the way you interpret negative events. Each time a negative thought arises, choose how to respond.*

> o *Challenge negative thoughts that are unfairly self-deprecating. Make sure your atmosphere is a positive one until you have your stability developed and stabilized.*

Breathe

> o *Try not to immediately react to any given situation. Stop, take a step back, and breathe. Ask yourself if it's worth it to get all worked up regarding the situation. See why this might be a trigger and choose to respond or react differently.*
>
> o *Be mindful of your thoughts, feelings, and actions. Investigate the deeper trigger and why it affects you in such a way. Remove the trigger and <u>nobody</u> can push your buttons.*

Take Care of You

> o *Love and care for yourself. Know what your de-stressors are and use them. They will take the edge off.*

- *Do simple things like getting a massage or exercise. Clear stress so there is no emotional mess.*

Get Back Up

- *We all lose it at times. We fly off the handle, get worked up, and even scream and cry. It happens to the best of us and it's okay! Apologize if needed and learn from it.*
- *Forgiveness is vital in our overall well-being. Most importantly, forgive yourself. Get back up, dust yourself off, and keep moving forward in the direction of wholeness.*

The Fruit of Emotional Stability

The fruit of your emotions will show and tell. The tree of stability will bear fruit. You will be tested (break through the soil) on your stability, but when the test comes, you will be grounded and able to stand still, and stay calm.

Think before you react, and your reaction won't be confusing, because you didn't react out of chaos. You can better handle setbacks and disappointments, because now you understand your triggers, and you think before you react.
You know how to adapt to change. You now know how to recognize and express your needs. You focus on resolution, and not the problem, because you have analyzed it. You learn from mistakes and constructive criticism.

You tend to see the larger perspective in a challenging situation. You can better handle emotional wounds such as failure, and rejection, but you recover quickly.

The power of emotional stability is centered around principle, faith, and confidence. If we practice these five principles along with faith and confidence, we will be able to better control and stabilize our emotions.

The principles are:

> o *self-awareness*
> o *self-control*
> o *adaptability*
> o *empathy*
> o *conflict management*

Self-awareness is the ability to recognize your own emotions, especially in the moment when they intensify quickly, and you seem to lose control.

Emotional self-awareness allows you to diffuse strong emotions long enough to realize why they are happening and prepare you for addressing them soberly with balance.

Self-control is knowing and recognizing where your emotions are and being able to manage them in a relatively calm manner.

Sometimes you have to walk away and take a deep breath, or let the situation go until you have fully thought it through and you are able to address it; without anger or if you need a minute to pray and get guidance as to how to handle the situation.

I intentionally placed prayer as a last option because most of the time when we are emotional, praying is the last thing we do or think about doing. The point is that your emotions can go from one to ten in a matter of seconds.

The power of your emotions if not governed, will make you react from the fleshly part of you, and everything you learned in Sunday school goes out the window. If you can maintain emotional control, you're much more likely not only to meet challenges concisely, but also execute godly principles. This way you will either introduce God or represent Him well.

Adaptability is like going with the flow, without getting too attached to any particular process, or outcome. The more adaptable you are, the easier you will be able take on the challenges of life.

Being empathetic means having the ability to see from the perspective of others; and respond naturally to their feelings. Right here is where you have to bring your emotions subject and depend totally on God.

The question becomes, how do I put my hurt aside to walk in the shoes of the person(s) that hurt me? How can I step outside my emotions to deal with their emotion(s)? Will empathy answer the question of why? Will this help me to process the hurt properly?

Empathy won't take away the hurt, but it will help you better understand where they are, where they are coming from, and why this occurred. Once this is established, you can now move into the five dimensions of hurt to see exactly where you are, and what you need to do to start the healing process.

Conflict management is the process of limiting the negative aspects of conflict while increasing the positive aspects of conflict. Whether at work, at home, or out in public, conflicts are inevitable. Therefore, being able to manage conflict is very necessary. Properly managed conflict can control the outcome.

The Power of Restoration

When you have conquered the power of forgiveness, the power of release, the power of emotional stability, now you can take on the power of restoration. When talking about restoration, you must address what was a certain way, disrupted and now it's ready to be in place again.

Let's deal with another aspect of your emotions. As you all know in life you sometimes make bad choices based on emotions. As a result of it, often times you lose stability in your emotions, you lose peace, joy, happiness and/or direction. You gain embarrassment, shame and you put a wall up to hide the fact that you messed up.

Rather than owning your decision or going to God in prayer, you play the blame game as the victim. From this aspect of emotional distress, you must deal with self. Ask me, I can attest to it. I've been there.

Acknowledgement to reality played a key role in moving forward from that place called stuck. I repented to God, forgave myself, and all parties involved. Once I did that, I could feel a shift in my life.

I began to labor in prayer regarding my next move, because although I was free, I needed to know how to move forward? God started restoring me from the inside. My emotions started to become stable, my heart wasn't heavy anymore, and because I forgave myself, I found that I had the capacity to release all parties involved. I took the wall down and the fear of moving forward dissipated.

Once you deal with self and own the decision that was made along with facing the facts that the results are real, then you can move onto forgiving, releasing, stabilizing, and positioning yourself for restoration. Once restoration is in motion, it provokes you to execute what you've learned.

The characteristics of the situation will show forth in the future, but this time because of what you've learned in the process to restoration, you can now identify it, and automatically jump into the position of execution mode of what you've learned from your past.

Therefore, you have a different perspective about the situation, and you not only think it through, but you pray for instructions and directions.

Now your experience along with knowledge and understanding has developed into wisdom. Aren't you grateful that God factored in the mistakes and bad decisions you would make when He created you?

The bible says in Joel 2:25 "And I will restore to you the years that the locust hath eaten, the cankerworm, and the caterpillar, and the palmerworm, my great army which I sent among you." God will also restore health unto you and heal your wounds according to Jeremiah 30:17. Restoration is one of the benefits we have as a kingdom citizen.

The Power of Love

Love is the greatest power of all powers. It has the ability to forgive, release, heal, restore, and cover. Love is pure and decent, innocent, and true. Love is as critical for your mind, and body as oxygen.

The more connected you are, the healthier you will be both physically and emotionally. Love is a strong emotion that is used as an expression of affection towards someone (I love you), or an expression of pleasure (I love ice cream) or an expression of human virtue that is based on compassion, and kindness.

Love is a state of being, that has nothing to do with something or someone outside yourself. The purest form of love. Love is unselfish and benevolent. It is self-directed and directed towards others.

Love improves self-esteem which causes you to take better self-care. Self-love increases the capacity of loving others.

Love is so powerful that there are (7) types of love that at one point or another in life, you will experience.

> - *Storage: natural affection, the love you share with your family.*
> - *Philia: the love that you have for friends.*
> - *Agape: this is the unconditional love, or divine love.*
> - *Ludus: this is playful love, like childish love or flirting.*
> - *Pragma: long standing love. The love in a marriage.*
> - *Philautia: the love of the self (negative or positive).*
> - *Eros: this is the love of romance, sexual or passionate.*

From a biblical perspective, 1 Peter 4:8 says: "Above all, have fervent and unfailing love for one another, because love covers a multitude of sins, it overlooks unkindness, and unselfishly seeks the best for others."

Love is a necessity in life; and in order to successfully operate in it, you have to forgive, and release. Remember, that life happens, and when it does, forgiveness and release add weight to love. The weight of the cross shows us how much Jesus loved us. He forgave us and died for us, that's love.

Memory is an Enemy to Forgiveness

The mind is a set of cognitive faculties including consciousness, perception, thinking, judgement, and memory. Memory is the faculty of the mind by which information is encoded, stored, and retrieved.

Often memory is understood as an informational processing system with explicit and implicit functioning. It is made up of a sensory processor, short term, and long-term memory.

The short-term memory recalls up to a minute without rehearsal. When the memory capacity is increased, it takes the information that it has received and groups it. This is called chunking. Chunking refers to an approach for making more efficient the use of short-term memory by grouping information. Chunking breaks up long strings of information into chunks.

Example, your telephone number is ten digits long, but you can remember it. Why? Because the memory takes the first three digits, groups it into what is known as an area code, then your memory groups the next three numbers followed by the last four numbers. We remember the number for a specific reason, but once the task is complete, we must look the number up again, unless the number is an important number to us.

This is how our memory works when we go through something, it groups the situation to the name(s) of the person(s) involved. If we deal with the emotion(s) of the situation at that moment, we will forgive quickly. If you don't deal with it, you give it permission to cross over into the long-term memory. Remember, short-term memory encodes information acoustically, meaning by hearing.

Long-term memory encodes it semantically. Semantic memory refers to a portion of long-term memory that processes ideas, and concepts that are not drawn from personal experience.

But there is another component to the long-term memory called episodic memory, "which attempts to capture information such as times, places, associated emotions, and other contextual who, what, when, where, and why knowledge. It is the collection of past individual experiences that occurred at a particular time and place. This is the part of the memory that can be an enemy to forgiveness, if not processed correctly.

To prevent this from happening means you have to acknowledge the hurt and process it through the five dimensions.

Forgive all parties involved, release it, stabilize your emotions, and experience the process of restoration. At this point your hurt is no longer a negative part of your life, it has now transitioned from hurt to healing. You have been equipped to help someone else out of their hurt just by giving your testimony.

In dealing with memory and emotions, you have to deal with the conscious, subconscious, and unconscious.

The conscious mind is your awareness now. You are aware of something on the outside as well as some specific mental functions happening on the inside.

The subconscious mind consists of accessible information. You can become aware of this information once you direct your attention to it. Think of this as a memory recall.

It is in charge of our recent memories; and is in continuous contact with the resources of the unconscious mind.

The unconscious mind is the storehouse of all memories and past experiences. Those that have been repressed through trauma, and those that have simply been consciously forgotten, and no longer important to us. It's from these memories and experiences that our beliefs, habits, and behaviors are formed.

The unconscious constantly communicates with the conscious mind through our subconscious. This is what provides us with the meaning to all our interactions which are filtered through our beliefs and habits. It communicates through feelings, emotions, imagination, sensations, and dreams.

Healed Perspective

Healed perspective is to become healthy, whole, or sound. To correct or put right. To restore, repair. To alleviate (distress). To get free from, to bring to an end, or conclusion.

An attitude toward, or a way of regarding something, a point of view. A way of regarding situations, facts, and judging their relative importance.

The proper or accurate point of view or the ability to see it, objectively. The ability to see it, know it, embrace it, and become it. It will <u>reveal</u>, <u>review</u>, <u>release</u>, <u>restore</u>, and <u>recover</u>.

Reveal the Hurt

There are two ways hurt is revealed, pre-and post. The first reveal is for your healing. Reveal, admit, and talk about the hurt, it will certainly afford you the opportunity to get healed. Don't just talk about one side of the hurt, but also talk about you, your part in the hurt, and response to the hurt.

Revealing your emotions will bring some level of liberty to the packed up baggage of the situation; thus, causing you to be able to position yourself to walk it out. Remember the more you talk it out will cause your emotions to prepare to release the toxins of the situation.

After you have been healed, and you have forgiven, and released; you can now experience a second reveal of the same hurt, except this time it is for someone else's healing.

Review the Hurt

In the healing process, you must review the situation in which the hurt occurred. Here is where you deal with raw emotions because you have to go back, and revisit not only the experience, but also all of the emotions tied to memories pertaining to the hurt.

The review process helps you to prepare for the healing process. The more you review, the more you identify the emotions. Now you are ready to analyze those emotions. Here is where you place the different emotions in the proper place, because when the situation happened your emotions where all over the place. This is the perfect place to look at your reaction to the action.

I know it hurt; I know you had a hard time believing this person was the one who caused the hurt. I know they were wrong; I know you can justify your feelings in this matter.

I know you were the victim, but in reviewing it, you then gain the power to release it, thus preventing you from becoming the villain.

Reviewing the hurt will take the sting out of the memory of it. Also, reviewing it will help you to see that forgiving and releasing them will take your power back from them.

Always analyze what they did and how they did it, and then ask yourself these questions: "is there a victim behind the villain? Is it worth allowing them to keep that power over me? Is it worth staying in prison emotionally? Will this keep me from seeing Jesus? Overall is it worth it?

Release the Hurt

You've revealed it, reviewed it, and now it's time to release it. You must release it from all aspects of your life. From your emotions, your soul, your mind, your spirit, and your heart.

How do I release the hurt? Weigh the hurt to see if there is a lesson that you can gain from the hurt. When you determine the lesson, ask how you can apply the lesson to your life so that the hurt will benefit you.

To successfully release the hurt, make sure you are accountable for your part in the hurt, whether is action or reaction. Taking responsibility for your part helps you to forgive; release yourself from the situation, and now you can better weigh other parties involved. It gives you ammunition against the enemy of your emotions, which is unforgiveness. Forgiveness is always for you, whether you are forgiving yourself or someone else.

Make sure you are accountable for your own emotions. Ask yourself, how did I handle the hurt? Was I open with the hurt? Or did I keep the hurt a secret? This will help you to forgive yourself. Why? Because how you processed the hurt determines the forgiveness factor. Remember, you have to forgive before you can release.

Make sure you have a tight strong support system that can help you dissect the hurt properly; especially during the time when your emotions are on a roller-coaster. Our emotions have highs and lows, so you need support to balance out those emotions. Remember, emotions are fickle, and they will fight against your decision to move forward in complete healing.

Restore after the Hurt

Restoration is inevitable after you forgive and release. Once restoration begins, you'll find out that you lost more than just power, but you also lost peace, trust, stability, and you. In the restoration process, God will make sure you are covered from shame and embarrassment.

Joel 2:25 – 27 says, And I will restore to you the years that the locust hath eaten, the cankerworm, and the caterpillar, and the palmerworm, my great army which I sent among you. And ye shall eat in plenty, and be satisfied, and praise the name of the LORD your God, that hath dealt wondrously with you: and my people shall never be ashamed. And ye shall know that I am in the midst of Israel, and that I am the LORD your God, and none else: and my people shall never be ashamed.

Recover from the Hurt

God will allow you to recover all with interest including time, trust, stability, and power. In the recovery process, don't make the mistake of looking for everything you had to return. When you recover you may not get the exact same thing, but God will give you new and better to replace the old. New friends, a new job and making more money. A new spouse with a different person or the same person with a mind and heart makeover.

Healed perspective is all about taking on a different point of view to walk through the proper process of healing. Remember, what you went through or what you are experiencing is not a surprise to God. He knew and knows, but you've got to trust Him and believe that it's going to work out in your favor. God is willing and able to do exceedingly and abundantly above all we could ever ask or think. His thoughts are not our thoughts and His ways are not our ways.

> *Jeremiah 29:11 says "For I know the plans and thoughts that I have for you,' says the LORD, 'plans for peace and well-being and not for disaster, to give you a future and a hope."*

It is all working for your good! The good, the bad and the ugly!

> *This is a good place to pray!!!*

Lord, thank you for loving me so much that you would give me instructions, directions, and time to change my perspective of the hurt that I have experienced.

Thank you for the knowledge, wisdom, and understanding of the hurt, and how to properly walk through the process of healing.

Lord cover my mind, heart, soul, and spirit, that I may be free of the fear of loving and trusting again. Help me to be open to love and live again. Moments may come, but I trust you in all things.

About the Author!

Atavia Barnes is the author of:

- *What My Smile Doesn't Tell You*
- *The Hurt that Helped*
- *#Catchit (Decide, Decree, Declare)*
- *Missing Pieces Administration Manual & Workbook*
- *Suits & Strategies Manual & Assessment Workbook*
- *The Providence Prayer Manual*

She serves in three capacities of the five-fold ministry: Prophet, Evangelist, and Teacher. The woman of God flows in a unique prophetic anointing that will captivate your spirit. She evangelizes for lost souls, and teaches Holiness.

Prophetess has a heart for God's people and is in search of who God is with a desire to know Him, not just about Him.

Relentless when seeking revelatory wisdom and understanding, she brings simplicity and balance in the lives of God's people for the betterment of Kingdom-living.

A Prayer Warrior, and Intercessor, who can and will pray. Her belief is "You must know the word to pray and you must pray the word to know."

Prophetess Barnes has an associate degree in Biblical Studies from the Jacksonville Theological Seminary, and a bachelor's degree in business administration with a concentration in Human Resources from American InterContinental University.

She is the CEO of:

- o *ASB Consulting Firm*
- o *ASB Collaborative*
- o *Suits & Strategies*
- o *Business & Bloom Coaching Services*

She is the proud mother of one son, Vékarious Ralphél Barnes, who is the Vice President of ASB Consulting Firm. He has a Bachelor of Science from Florida State University in Chemistry with a minor in Physics and Mathematics. Also, he has a master's degree from the University of Florida, in Pharmaceutical Chemistry.

Prophetess Barnes has a full life that she enjoys daily simply because she allows her faith to control her atmosphere.

References

4 Signs Someone Is Suffering From Emotional Distress. (2016, September 29). Retrieved from Power of Positivity: https://www.powerofpositivity.com/emotional-distress/

5 Comonents of Emotional Intelligence. (2021, March 04). Retrieved from Institute for Integrative Nutrition: https://www.integrativenutrition.com/blog/2016/11/5-essential-principles-of-emotional-intelligence

7 Effective Ways to Deal with Rejection in Relationships. (2018, November 23). Retrieved from Dumb Little Man: https://www.dumblittleman.com/7-effective-ways-to-deal-with-rejection/

Catron, A. (2017, December 06). What Is Love? A Philosophy of Life. Retrieved from Huffpost: http://www.huffingtonpost.com/adrian-catron/what-is-love-a-philosophy_b_5697322.html

Episodic Memory. (2021, March 02). Retrieved from Wikipedia : https://en.wikipedia.org/wiki/Episodic_memory

Genesis 1:26. (n.d.). Retrieved from Bible Gateway: https://www.biblegateway.com/passage/?search=Genesis+1%3A26&version=KJV

Jax, C. (2020). How Do Words Hurt People? Retrieved from Classroom: https://classroom.synonym.com/words-hurt-people-12104.html

Leary, M. P. (2020, April 28). Physical and Psychological Pain: The Case of Hurt Feelings. Retrieved from The Great Courses Daily:

https://www.thegreatcoursesdaily.com/physical-and-psychological-pain-the-case-of-hurt-feelings/

Loneliness. (2021, March 07). Retrieved from Wikipedia: https://en.wikipedia.org/wiki/Loneliness

McGrath, E. (2002, December 01). The Power of Love. Retrieved from Psychology Today: https://www.psychologytoday.com/articles/200212/the-power-love

Memory. (2021, February 27). Retrieved from Wikipedia: https://en.wikipedia.org/wiki/Memory

Merriam-Webster Since 1828. (2021). Retrieved from Merriam-Webster.com: https://www.merriam-webster.com/dictionary/hurt

Mind. (2021, February 15). Retrieved from Wikipedia: https://en.wikipedia.org/wiki/Mind

O'Connor, B. (n.d.). Pucker Mob. Retrieved from Pucker Mob: https://www.puckermob.com/lifestyle/8-easy-practices-that-will-help-you-be-emotionally-stable/

Paleologos, M. (2014, January 25). The Power of Love. Retrieved from Huffpost: http://www.huffingtonpost.com/mary-paleologos/love-and-relationships_b_4300010.html

Reject. (2021). Retrieved from Dictionary. Cambridge: https://dictionary.cambridge.org/dictionary/english/reject

Rejection. (n.d.). Retrieved from http://www.isob-bible.org/innerheal/InnerHealset/Session-Three.Html

Romans 4:17. (n.d.). Retrieved from Bible Gateway: https://www.biblegateway.com/passage/?search=Romans+4%3A17&version=KJV

Rumination (psychology). (2021, February 08). Retrieved from Wikipedia: https://en.wikipedia.org/wiki/Rumination_(psychology)

Tanoos, T. (2013, December 01). Power of prayer boosts self-control and emotional stability. Retrieved from Emax Health: https://www.emaxhealth.com/11400/prayer-boosts-self-control-and-emotional-stability

Tarbox, P. (n.d.). 10 Indicators a Spirit of Rejection is Tormenting You. Retrieved from Above & Beyond Christian Counseling: http://aandbcounseling.com/10-indicators-spirit-of-rejection-tormenting/

Thaik, C. (2013, July 06). Love Heals! Retrieved from Huffpost: http://www.huffingtonpost.com/dr-cynthia-thaik/love-health-benefits_b_3131370.html

The Free Dictionary. (2021). Retrieved from The Free Dictionary: http://www.thefreedictionary.com/word+meaning

The Power of Love. (2016, June 09). Retrieved from Psychology Today: https://www.psychologytoday.com/articles/200212/the-power-love

Wehrenberg, M. P. (2016, April 20). Rumination: A Problem in Anxiety and Depression. Retrieved from Psychology Today: https://www.psychologytoday.com/blog/depression-management-techniques/201604/rumination-problem-in-anxiety-and-depression

Winch, G. (2015, December 8). Why rejection hurts so much — and what to do about it. Retrieved from Ideas.Ted.Com: https://ideas.ted.com/why-rejection-hurts-so-much-and-what-to-do-about-it/

Winch, G. P. (2015, January 06). 10 Surprising Facts About Failure. Retrieved from Psychology Today: https://www.psychologytoday.com/blog/the-squeaky-wheel/201501/10-surprising-facts-about-failure

Winch, G. P. (2015, June 04). 7 Characteristics of Emotionally Strong People. Retrieved from Psychology Today: https://www.psychologytoday.com/blog/the-squeaky-wheel/201506/the-7-characteristics-emotionally-strong-people

Zimmermann, K. A. (2014, January 29). Semantic Memory: Definition & Examples. Retrieved from Live Science: https://www.livescience.com/42920-semantic-memory.html

www.ingramcontent.com/pod-product-compliance
Lightning Source LLC
Chambersburg PA
CBHW070511090426
42735CB00012B/2740